CALIFORNIA MURALS

JAN 1984

CALIFORNIA MURALS

Conceived and Written by
Yoko Clark and Chizu Hama
Photographed by
Marshall Gordon

Lancaster—Miller Publishers Berkeley, California 1979

Other titles in the Lancaster - Miller Art Series:

Colored Reading
The Graphic Art of
Frances Butler
ISBN 0-89581-011-5

Dragons and Other Creatures
Chinese Embroidery
by Katherine Westphal
ISBN 0-89581-012-3

Mel Ramos: Watercolors
ISBN 0-89581-009-3

Buttons: Art in Miniature
by Stefan O. Schiff
ISBN 0-89581-013-1

The Mad Monk
by Lewis Lancaster
ISBN 0-89581-017-4

Copyright © 1979 Lancaster-Miller Inc.
3165 Adeline St.,
Berkeley, California 94703

ISBN 0-89581-106-0

Library of Congress Catalog No. 79-91012

Acknowledgement is made to Mr. and Mrs. Clyde L. Juchau
for assistance in the production of this book.

CONTENTS

PREFACE AND ACKNOWLEDGEMENTS

We have worked on this book about California murals for more than a year. Our original intention was to publish a book in Japan, to introduce the Japanese public to the mural works of California, hopefully to get them excited about murals, so that they would start painting walls themselves.

During this year, we collected nearly 1,500 color slides, challenged by the task of reducing a hundred-foot painted wall to a six-and-a-half-inch photograph, still conveying its emotional impact. The photographic problem was compounded by the different architectural surfaces on which murals are painted: stairs, doors, windows, and electrical wiring.

In selecting photographs for this book, we chose many close-up pictures. We intended to show the texture of the walls and the brush strokes. We attempted to choose those pictures of greatest human interest. For instance, the picture of the enormous face of Strother Martin with an old man walking in front of it conveys not only the size of the mural, but also demonstrates its integral function in the neighborhood.

We thank all artists whose works we have included in this book, and also those whose art we were not able to include but who lent support to our project. While the authors remain responsible for the content of all the written material in this book, information for the captions was collected during interviews with the artists. We would like to acknowledge these people to whom we feel particularly indebted in the preparation of the book: Tim Drescher, Gary Graham, Osha Neumann, Jane Norling, Ray Patlan, Patricia Rodrigues, Terry Schoonhover, Stefan, Kent Twitchell, and John Wehrle.

We also wish to give photo credit to Tim Drescher for "The Fire Next Time," to Stephen Keachie for "Dutch Boy," and to Craig Kolb for "People's History of Telegraph Avenue."

Finally, our special thanks to Janet King for her editorial assistance; and to Rich Clark, Susan Gordon, and Edd Myers for their encouragement in the preparation of this book.

October, 1979

Yoko Clark
Chizu Hama
Marshall Gordon

INTRODUCTION

Shortly after our move from Japan to Berkeley in 1974, we encountered a huge painting, covering the entire side wall of a paint store on a busy corner of University Avenue. It was like nothing we had ever seen in Japan, for in addition to its enormity and content, it engrossed us with its commingling of reality and illusion. This "Dutch Boy" mural (later whitewashed by the building's new owner) showed a view of San Francisco Bay as seen from the freeway in Berkeley. The scene was painted as if observed through the white smoke emitted from a real-life chimney. In this painting, the real and the imaginary were blended, and the observer soon lost sight of the difference. This mural was dramatically different from paintings customarily viewed in galleries and museums. It seemed to zoom from its confining physical limit directly into the street, grabbing the viewer's attention.

Visionary murals, with tones fanciful and fantastic, imaginary and speculative, cover numerous walls of California buildings. Born in the 60s, they were encouraged by the surrealistic school of art and the blossoming psychedelic culture of the day. And California's permissive attitude has provided fertile soil in which this new art form might grow. The emergence of the first mural in San Francisco illustrates this eloquently. In the mid-60s, the Haight-Ashbury district was a haven for "flower children." Free rock concerts were given in neighboring Golden Gate Park. Mural art was born to the accompaniment of the music, as local painters participated in public "chalk-ins" on the asphalt strip in the center of the park. From these early expressions grew a more permanent and public artistic medium: murals. In Haight-Ashbury in 1967, an unknown woman artist painted the first fantastic mural, depicting the evolutionary cycle of mineral, plant, and animal life.

In the following years, murals of diverse styles, contents, and messages were painted throughout San Francisco. In the Mission district, Chicano and Latin artists, including the Mujeres Muralistas group, Michael Rios, and others, painted colorful murals, reflecting their cultural heritages and incorporating Aztec and other pre-Hispanic designs into their work. Their murals show the influence of the great Mexican muralists Siqueiros, Orozco and Rivera, in their dynamic perspective.

Local residents became involved in these projects, supplying funding, materials, or moral support, often assisting the artists in preparing the walls or in the actual execution of the murals. These community murals adorn many once dreary working-class and minority neighborhood walls, frequently imparting poignant, militant criticism of existing political and economic conditions.

"Black History Panel" in San Francisco's George Washington High School, was completed in 1973 by Dewey Crumpler, a black artist. The mural came into being when politically active black students insisted that the existing mural (a 1930s WPA rendition of George Washington's life) be replaced with one more relevant to current sociopolitical conditions. Dewey, a high-school student when the near-riot demands began, was a college graduate when he finally completed the panel, six years later.

In East Los Angeles in 1973, self-taught Chicano artist Charles "Gato" Felix and his friends started to paint the row of drab, grey, graffiti-defiled walls of the Estrada Court Housing Project. The artists were soon joined by more than a hundred Mexican-American housing-project residents, ranging in age from young children to adolescents to grandmothers. Equally important, the artists succeeded in channeling the potentially hostile energy of barrio gang members to an activity that was positive, creative, cooperative, and a source of great pride.

The renaissance of the American mural movement was made possible by the freedom that American youth struggled for and won in the last decade. Many artists had felt alienated from museums and galleries, where they experienced frustration when their art was rejected according to the arbitrary standards made by elitist galleries and their critics in New York. The social upheavals encouraged artists to get out of the studios and into the streets.

One day in 1969, three Venice California artists decided to paint the side wall of a building near their house. They painted an image of the view across from the wall so that after seeing the real view down the street, one would turn around and look back up the street to see the same view again, only painted on the side of a building. The Los Angeles Fine Arts Squad was thus born of the desire to bring fantastic art back where they believed it belonged—on the streets, for everyone to see and enjoy. Their mural, one of the earliest visionary works in Los Angeles, motivated other artists to forsake their studios and become muralists.

Osha Neumann was an avant-garde studio painter in New York in the 60s, who became disillusioned by what he thought to be the self-destructive direction in which avant-garde art was heading. He decided to give up painting altogether and withdrew into the serenity of a mountain commune. A few years later, while walking in San Francisco, the sight of the murals in the Mission district inspired him to become a muralist. Later he became director/artist of the Berkeley mural, "People's History of Telegraph Avenue."

One of the difficulties that murals face is destruction by whitewashing or repainting of the walls, most likely to occur when a building changes hands. The "Dutch Boy" is a casualty of this sort, though there are numerous others. As a preventive measure, artists might secure an agreement with the owner of the building before painting begins, guaranteeing that they be informed of ownership changes, and requiring their consent in order to repaint the walls.

In recent years, mural painting has spread to other parts of the world. Mexico and Chile have a strong tradition of mural painting, but a grass-roots mural movement is now spreading rapidly on the European continent. In Japan, within the past five years, murals have been seen adorning walls in a few big cities. Most of them are painted on commercial sites, such as large department stores, coffee shops, and boutiques. Non-commercial community murals are rare, however, as traffic ordinances restrict the potentially distracting decoration of walls. Japanese muralists are trying to find ways to overcome this restriction, to make murals more prevalent.

The potential of the mural movement is enormous as a vibrant new medium by which visual art can be expressed. Unlimited room exists for new thematic, stylistic, and compositional explorations, and a vast number of walls await painting.

THE PLATES

PEOPLE'S HISTORY OF TELEGRAPH AVENUE
(detail)

ARTISTS:	Osha Neumann, Janet Kranzberg, Brian Thiele, Daniel Galvez
LOCATION:	Telegraph and Haste streets, Berkeley
YEAR:	1976 (6 months)
DIMENSIONS:	16' x 88'
MEDIUM:	Politec paint
FUNDING:	Artists' and peoples' contributions

This mural, on the corner of Telegraph Avenue and Haste Street, three blocks from the University campus, covers what locals refer to as the "People's Wall." The artists incorporated scenes from the 1964 "Free Speech Movement," Vietnamese anti-war demonstrations, the 1969 "Third World Strike," the 1969 community-police confrontation and ensuing creation of "People's Park," and the psychedelic movement of the 70s into this lively mural on which forty people volunteered their talent and hundreds donated money. This mural has become an unofficial peoples' monument to the City of Berkeley, and bears the inscription, "This project is supported by your contribution."

MONUMENT TO STROTHER MARTIN (detail)

ARTIST: Kent Twitchell
LOCATION: Fountain and Kingsley streets, Hollywood
YEAR: 1972 (1 year, working spare time)
DIMENSIONS: 12' x 45'
MEDIUM: Enamel house paint
FUNDING: Commissioned by the building owner

"It is a stream of consciousness painting. I did not begin with a definite design. I was developing the image and the color as I went on painting," says artist Kent Twitchell. The mural is a dedication to Strother Martin, an actor in "The Wild Bunch." As the mural was being painted, the actor heard about it and came to the site to pose. The artist explains that this mural is one from a series entitled "Monument to American Cultural Heroes." "Nowadays," says Twitchell, "it is not in vogue to think in terms of heroes, but when I grew up, I was always fascinated by them." Kent Twitchell's interest is in portraying modern-day heroes who, at unexpected moments, reveal our own heroic characteristics.

OCEANIA

ARTISTS: Gary Graham (artist/composer), Edgar Monroe (designer),
                          Lou Silva, Tod Stanton
LOCATION: O'Farrell Theater, O'Farrell and Polk streets, San Francisco
YEAR: 1979 (4 months)
DIMENSIONS: 30' x 80' (front wall); 40' x 80' (back wall);
                          140' x 35' (sides)
MEDIUM: Show and display acrylic paint
FUNDING: Commissioned by theater owner

This mural, a celebration of the ocean, mixes realistic images with such fantastic elements as sunken cities of ancient times; an underwater pyramid, reminiscent of the last continent of Atlantis; Neptune, Roman god of the sea; and a mermaid. Some of the sea animals depicted here are real creatures; some are exaggerated in their sizes, while others are pure fantasy. "Oceania" is a repaint of the artists' former mural on the same building, which had faded badly since its completion in 1972.

UNTITLED (detail)

ARTIST: Timothy Jenk
LOCATION: Polk and Washington streets, San Francisco
YEAR: 1974 (2 months)
DIMENSIONS: 20' x 100'
MEDIUM: Laytex house paint
FUNDING: Private

At this busy San Francisco intersection, artist Timothy Jenk created an old-fashioned country scene, in marked contrast to its urban surroundings. This fantastic house is complete with painted balcony, windows, ivy leaves, and potted geraniums; and a Model-A Ford's headlight cleverly disguises the building's actual electrical meter. A father and son load the car with fresh fruit and vegetables as the mother and daughter pass by the side wall of the house. This peaceful country scene, in which swans gracefully adorn a lake in the foreground, presents a dream-like setting in which people might envision themselves as they go about their business.

LA RAZA (detail)

ARTISTS: Daniel Galvez, Stephanie Barrett, Brian Theile, Osha Neumann
LOCATION: Adeline and Alcatraz Streets, Berkeley
YEAR: 1977 (4 months)
DIMENSIONS: 70' x 15'
MEDIUM: Enamel paint
FUNDING: CETA grant, $200 donation from the Goodwill store

The flamboyant style of Chicano artist Daniel Galvez and friends converted the side wall of the Goodwill store into a multi-colored gigantic semitruck, moving under clear blue skies. The painting merges with the real California sky above. Combining a traditional Mexican theme with more contemporary subject matter, the detail shown here is of a powerful female figure, based on "Democracy Freeing Herself" by Mexican master muralist D.A. Siqueiros. Beneath her, Mexican and American farm workers march, led by organizer Caesar Chavez. To the right, in a yellow smock, on a ladder, is Diego Rivera, painting a mural about the Mexican Revolution. The funeral ceremony is probably to honor a slain member of the United Farm Workers' Union.

PING YUEN MURAL (detail)

ARTIST: Josie Grant
LOCATION: Ping Yuen Housing Project, China Town, San Francisco
YEAR: 1979 (2½ years)
DIMENSIONS: 20' x 165' (five walls of the two-story housing project)
MEDIUM: Politec paint
FUNDING: Salary from CETA
                  Material from Office of Comjunity Development and the
                  San Francisco Planning Commission

Federal CETA funding enabled Josie Grant to decorate a housing project in China Town. She transferred her mural design of Chinese zodiac characters, symbols, and landscape onto a sunrise sky background of extremely rich coloring. Beneath the California morning sunshine, mellow-faced gods sit or stand on the clouds while animals play cheerfully around the Chinese landscape. Josie, an energetic artist, spent eight hours every weekday for two and a half years painting this mural. As she worked, local residents stopped by to admire the results. The theme of this mural is familiar to the old Chinese immigrants, and the younger generation may come to appreciate their ancestors' culture through the visual impact of this mural.

FALL OF ICARUS

ARTIST: John Wehrle
LOCATION: Windward Avenue, Venice
YEAR: 1978 (5 months)
DIMENSIONS: 20' x 90'
MEDIUM: Oil paint
FUNDING: $4,800 grant from California Art Council

John Wehrle, who lives in Montana, chose a wall facing the Pacific Ocean in Venice, California, on which to execute this project. His "Fall of Icarus," based on the Greek myth, is a portrait of Los Angeles, viewed before its development.

His mural shows a view of the cactus-covered desert, framed by gently sloping mountains. In this unlikely setting appears a drive-in theater marquee, announcing the title, "Fall of Icarus." Two cowboys and three angels watch the giant screen on which an astronaut falls through space. The observer who parks his car in the lot directly in front of the mural is instantly transported into this drive-in theater in the middle of the desert.

ST. CHARLES PAINTING (detail)

ARTIST: Los Angeles Fine Arts Squad (Terry Schoonhoven)
LOCATION: St. Charles Place Apartment Building, Windward and Speedway
                 streets, Venice
YEAR: 1979 (11 months)
DIMENSIONS: 52' x 102'
MEDIUM: Enamel paint
FUNDING: $5,000 Grant from California Arts Council

Is the bicycle rider going into the fantasy world beyond the gray wall? The painting on this Venice, California apartment seems to be a continuation of the real sidewalk. Terry comments on his art: "I like painting in Los Angeles. It almost has to be in L.A. for me to do the kind of murals I want to paint. The air is thick and light and sometimes hazy, allowing me to paint a dreamlike world. L.A. is a movie town and the whole place gives an impression of being in a movie. In 'St. Charles Painting,' a mirror image of the view across the street, I did not include any people. An urban setting without people might suggest an environmental catastrophe. But I want to leave the interpretation open to people's speculation. The image here is calm and quiet with no implication of violence. I didn't mean to be prophetic. I thought it would be more mysterious."

SAN FRANCISCO AS SEEN FROM BERKELEY (detail)

ARTIST: Stefen
LOCATION: University and Milvia, Berkeley
YEAR: 1974 (200 hours) Destroyed: 1977
DIMENSIONS: 90' x 25'
MEDIUM: Latex house paint
FUNDING: Material from the Dutch Boy Paint Store and the artist

Popularly known as "The Dutch Boy Mural," this visionary work was a favorite Berkeley landmark until it was callously destroyed by a new owner of the building. The artist created a collage of reality and fantasy in this view west from Berkeley across the San Francisco Bay. The mural's divided freeways stretching across to San Francisco seem to lead to another world, while the stage, footlights, and curtains add yet another layer of reality to the fascinating picture. The life-size Dutch Boy figure, a portrait of the artist, heightens the contrast between reality and illusion.

LATÍNOAMERICA (detail)

ARTISTS: Mujeres Muralistas (Irene Perez, Patricia Rodrigues,
                 Graciela Carillo, Consuelo Mendez)
LOCATION: Mission Model Cities, Mission and 25th streets, San Francisco
YEAR: 1974 (3 months)
MEDIUM: Politec paint
FUNDING: $1,000 commission from Mission Model Cities

The mural depicts motifs borrowed from Venezuela, Mexico, Peru, Guatemala, and Bolivia. Painted on the parking lot wall of Mission Model Cities, the mural shows diverse aspects of Latin American life, including mothers and their children, and Venezuelan and Bolivian devil figures. Mission Model Cities is a neighborhood group that assists the community in legal and social issues. "Although the mural's central message is self-determination of Chicano and Latin people," a Mujeres Muralistas member says, "the painting does not employ harsh political images, which sometimes are used for political murals done by male muralists." Instead, it is a full-scale ode to life, expressed in more feminine symbols—sensitivity, nurturing and cooperation. The detail picture shown here is a portrait of two Latin American women embodying innate beauty and cultural pride.

ACORN MURAL

ARTIST: George Mead (designer), Mike Hardeman, Claire Freitas,
                            Ivor Heskett (painters)
LOCATION: Cathedral Building, downtown Oakland
YEAR: 1976 (3 months to design; 10 days for painting)
DIMENSION: 90' x 35'
MEDIUM: Oil paint
FUNDING: National Paint and Coating Association
                            Artist won a contest over 60 competitors

This mural is striking because of its size and location. It is viewed by thousands of people working or shopping in the downtown Oakland area and can be seen for miles. Designed as part of the renovation of the City of Oakland, this mural portrays a huge acorn sprouting three healthy leaves and a long, vital root. The oak sprout grows up to the dawn sky above the downtown silhouette, while the root grows down through water and soil, as well as through other materials symbolic of the life of the people. The oak tree, symbol of Oakland, appears to grow from a balance of nature and people.

BEAVER MOUNTAIN (detail)

ARTIST: Timothy Jank
LOCATION: Apartment house, Ord and 18th streets, San Francisco
YEAR: 1974 (3 months)
DIMENSIONS: 25' x 120' (A wrap-around mural of a two-story
                 apartment house)
MEDIUM: Laytex paint
FUNDING: Commissioned by the owner of the house

A young San Francisco apartment-house owner saw some murals while traveling through Switzerland and decided to have his property similarly adorned. He selected a muralist from respondents to an advertisement placed with the San Francisco Art Institute. Though commissioned to paint a Rocky Mountain scene, the muralist envisioned an African jungle, and the two motifs were combined in an interesting blend. While the work was still in progress, muralist and patron agreed to expand the painting, which resulted in a mural wrapping completely around the house.

WINDS OF CHANGE

ARTISTS:	Osha Neumann (designer), Daniel Galvez, Brian Thiele
LOCATION:	Co-op Credit Union, Sacramento and University, Berkeley
YEAR:	1977 (3 months)
DIMENSIONS:	135' x 21'
MEDIUM:	Politec paint
FUNDING:	$2,500 grant from Co-op Credit Union

In "Winds of Change" gigantic, colorful birds fly into the mural and out of it. The birds carry working-class people into the mural to fight the spread of mechanization, symbolized by men with heads of a television set, an oil barrel, a banker's briefcase, a hamburger, and a computer, all dressed in suits and ties. The birds sweep away these symbols of twentieth century corruption. In this detail, the mural appears to be flowing with birds, which seem to fly right over the spectators' heads.

OUR HISTORY IS NO MYSTERY (detail)

ARTISTS: Haight Ashbury Muralists (Jane Norling, Miranda Bergman,
                  Vicky Hamlin, Peggy Tucker, Arch Williams, Thomas Kunz)
LOCATION: John Adams Community College, Masonic and Hayes streets,
                  San Francisco
YEAR: 1976 (10 months)
DIMENSIONS: 8' x 300'
MEDIUM: Politec Paint
FUNDING: Haight Street Beautification Revenue Sharing Fund

Painted as part of the Bicentennial commemoration, this mural celebrates the history of San Francisco from the standpoint of the working people. It is an unofficial story of San Francisco's development. The beginning portion of the mural portrays American Indian life, and shows Japanese people being sent to internment camps during World War II. The detail picture shows a grim-faced old man, a shoe polisher, serving a man with a cigar, clothed in his business suit. In this partial view of the street scene from the 1934 San Francisco general strike, the long line of people wait to purchase groceries.

TRINITY (detail)

ARTIST: Kent Twitchell
LOCATION: Otis Art Institute, Wilshire Boulevard, Los Angeles
YEAR: 1977 (9 months)
DIMENSIONS: 40' x 56'
MEDIUM: Nova acrylic paint
FUNDING: $1,500 CETA grant

While a student at the Otis Art Institute in Los Angeles, Kent Twitchell began to paint the school's wall, at artist Charles White's suggestion. Eventually "Trinity" became Kent's project to obtain his Master in Fine Arts Degree. The mural is an ultra-modern version of a religious painting, "blown up on a government building," for.the school was then owned by Los Angeles County. The mural was designed after "Trinity" by Renaissance master Masaccio, although the modern painter did not use any of the familiar religious iconography. Instead, there are two contemporary symbols merged with the traditional Holy Family. First, all of them are clad in the white gowns of the medical profession, suggesting that doctors are the modern-day wise men. Second, the figures are Hollywood T.V. series characters from the 50s and 60s. The painting is an American monument to television culture.

UNTITLED (detail)

ARTIST:	Walter Killion
LOCATION:	Telegraph Community Center, Telegraph and 53rd streets, Oakland
YEAR:	1978 (3 months)
DIMENSIONS:	45' x 15'
MEDIUM:	Exterior enamel paint
FUNDING:	Alameda County Welfare Department and Telegraph Community Center

The mural was painted by a welfare worker on the wall of the Telegraph Community Center, an organization sponsored primarily by the Southern Baptist Convention. People of different ages, racial origins and social backgrounds are shown participating in such diverse Center activities as dances, therapy, field trips, Bible classes, recycling projects, and sharing meals. Representing actual Center participants, the figures in the mural are shown in a therapy dance session designed to help people with emotional and social problems.

THE SPIRIT OF YOUTH IN AMERICA

ARTIST:	Charles Lobdell
LOCATION:	The Paltenghi Youth Center, Haight-Ashbury district, San Francisco
YEAR:	1977 (11 months)
MEDIUM:	Politec paint
FUNDING:	San Francisco Art Commission, design competition winner

During the 60s and 70s in San Francisco's Haight-Ashbury district, painters joining in the street celebrations translated their concepts and visions into a permanent form, as public mural art. Among the abundant Haight-Ashbury murals, "The Spirit of Youth in America" is striking for its size and content. Under a canopy of stars and galaxies, the Founding Fathers, American Indian Chief Joseph, Martin Luther King, Jr., presidents Kennedy and Truman, a geodesic dome, and a woman figure symbolizing liberation and freedom, interact with youths in this lively mural.

MONARCH (detail)

ARTIST: Kent Twitchell
LOCATION: Monarch Bridal and Tuxedo, Broadway and 2nd streets,
               Los Angeles
YEAR: 1971 (sketch); 1973 (groom painted); 1974 (bride painted)
DIMENSIONS: 70' x 70'
MEDIUM: Sinclair house paint

In Latin culture, a wedding is a gala celebration promoting a man and a woman to the status of cultural heroes. This mural is a representational picture of the owner of the tuxedo business, Carlos Ortiz, and his girl friend. Originally designed to cover only the lower two stories of the building, the mural sketch pleased Carlos so much that he had the muralist paint the entire five-story building. Artist Kent Twitchell states that he painted in a blue monotone to give the mural a non-commercial appearance. The bride and groom in the mural do not appear ecstatic, nor are they particularly glamorous; they look like "real people."

RAINBOW PEOPLE (detail)

ARTISTS:	Haight Ashbury Muralists (Jane wnorling, Miranda Bergman, Selma Brown, Thomas Kunz, Peggy Tucker, Arch Williams)
LOCATION:	Haight Ashbury district, San Francisco
YEAR:	1974 (4 months)
DIMENSIONS:	20' x 8'
MEDIUM:	Politec paint
FUNDING:	Donations and artists' own money

The Haight Ashbury Muralists originally painted this mural to commemorate the Haight Street Anti-Vietnam War march in October, 1972. The artists converted one of the many local boarded-up storefronts into a visual statement, adding beauty and color to the neighborhood. This detail shows the 1972 Haight Street march in which 6,000 neighborhood people participated. The rally marches along the cleaned-up, car-free Haight Street, lead by the San Francisco Mime Troup. In 1974, when the painting started to chip away, the residents encouraged the artists to repaint the mural.

PARA EL MERCADO (detail)

ARTISTS: Mujeres Muralistas (Graciela Carillo, Consuelo Mendez)
LOCATION: Paco's Tacos, South Van Ness and 24th streets, San Francisco
YEAR: 1974
MEDIUM: Politec paint
FUNDING: Commissioned by Paco's Tacos

News of the planned opening of a McDonald's in the Latin American Mission District of San Francisco posed a threat to the neighborhood's small ethnic restaurants. In response to this threat, two members of Mujeres Muralistas, formed by Chicana women, painted the wall of Paco's taco stand, appealling to Mission residents to support local businesses and eat tacos instead of hamburgers. The entire painting depicts Latin American people from ancient and modern times engaged in various food-related activities. In this detail, a boy holding a parrot waits for his mother to finish shopping, while an enormous owl watches.

SONG OF UNITY

ARTISTS: Ray Patlan, Brian Theile, Osha Neumann, Anna de Leon
LOCATION: Restaurant "La Pena," Prince and Shattuck, Berkeley
YEAR: 1978 (6 months)
DIMENSIONS: 15' x 40'
MEDIUM: Politec paint, ceramic and papier mache (reliefs)

The interior of the Berkeley restaurant "La Pena" is decorated with indigenous South American artifacts. La Pena functions as both restaurant and cultural center, where Latin American movies, slide shows, lectures, concerts, and poetry readings take place. The unique feature of the mural shown is its combination of flat-surface painting with reliefs, imparting the mural with dynamic three-dimentional appeal. The papier mache relief forms the face and hands of the late Victor Jara, internationally reknown Chilean singer, killed in the 1973 coup d'état. Victor's hands were cut off by executioners in front of a large crowd, as punishment for playing protest songs in support of the Allende government.

THE FIRE NEXT TIME

ARTIST: Dewey Crumpler
LOCATION: Joseph Lee Recreation Center, Bay View at Hunter's Point,
                  San Francisco
YEAR: 1977 (9 months)
DIMENSIONS: 35' x 48'
MEDIUM: Politec paint
FUNDING: Grants from San Francisco Art Commission and CETA

Dewey Crumpler grew up in the Hunter's Point community. "I used to play in the gym here. I always dug this wall space and I wanted to put something about the beauty of the community people here. The fire is very significant as a subject matter because in black mythology, it doesn't have any negative connotation. It means rebirth, strength and struggle." The mural is divided into three sections. The right side deals with culture—arts, dance, and music; religion is the theme of the center piece; education is the subject of the left section. At the top of the mural are sonofu birds, agricultural gods in black mythology, who bring forth plentiful crops. Paul Robeson and Harriet Tubman are shown in the two circles.

ancisco

ARTIST: John Wehrle
LOCATION: Gilman and Sante Fe avenues, Albany, California
DIMENSIONS: 13' x 62'
MEDIUM: oil paint
YEAR: 1979
FUNDING: Commissioned by Toot Sweets Bakery

This twentieth-century American landscape, adorning the wall of a neighborhood bakery, blends a familiar East Bay scene with elements of fantasy. Egrets migrating across the Emeryville mudflats share the scene with impromptu wood sculptures, actually present when the painting was begun, while a man tumbles from out of nowhere. The far left portion of the mural, not seen in this view, shows a freeway sign with the word, "ancisco" just visible. The missing portion, "San Fr" lends a realistic tone to the image—if the viewer can decifer this puzzle. Denying any deeper message in his mural, artist John Wehrle suggests that people gain whatever meaning they will from its visual symbols.

OCEANUS

ARTIST:	Gary Graham (class instructor), Edgar Monroe, Lou Silva, Tod Stanton, Lois Fischer (designers) and 40 students of Laney Community College's Mural Workshop
LOCATION:	Freeway underpass at Hudson and Claremont Avenues, Oakland
YEAR:	1977–78
DIMENSIONS:	15′ x 150′
MEDIUM:	Politec paint
FUNDING:	Material paid for by Peralta Community College District; executed with the permission of California Transportation Department

This imposing mural was created as a result of the cooperation between artists, state agencies, and the North Oakland community. The California Transportation Department gave permission for the artists to use a portion of this Highway 24 underpass to communicate an ecological message of great importance to the artists.

The mural depicts a scene from the Farallon Islands, off of San Francisco, looking West towards the Bay. Shown are a host of lovely sea creatures, threatened by chemical and nuclear wastes from American industry. In the unseen portion of the mural, a research boat and divers investigate these toxic pollutants, attempting to restore the ecological balance to the Ocean. The unnatural-looking flora adorning the ocean floor represent strange new species forming as a result of actual leakage from several barrels of plutonium deposited off the Farallon Islands.

UNDERPASS ABSTRACT

ARTIST: Gary Graham and Lois Fischer (designers) plus Peralta
Community College students

LOCATION: Freeway underpass at 51st Street and Telegraph Avenue,
Oakland

YEAR: 1978

DIMENSIONS: 30' x 20'

MEDIUM: Acrylic paint

FUNDING: Materials paid for by Peralta Community College District;
executed with the permission of the California
Transportation Department

This vibrant mural, enlivening the otherwise dull grey surface of a freeway underpass, is also the product of an out-of-the-classroom student team effort. The striking shapes in this abstract mural were designed to lift the viewer's spirits as he drives familiar neighborhood roads.

This book was set in Universe typefaces
by Mergenthaler Photocomposition at Holmes Typographers,
San Jose; and printed at Grafiche Editoriali Ambrosiane
S.p.A., Milan, Italy.